PARADISE STATE OF MIND

by Amal Maow

In the name of Allah, the most Compassionate, the most Merciful

Content

Table of Contents

About

Within every human there are three components. The ruuh (soul), the nafs (soul+body), and the jism (body). Knowing each part of yourself is essential to increasing the quality of your life, that way both your blessings and struggles in life will make sense to you. When you know who you are and where you come from, there is a sense of security and confidence you will maintain within you that no one can take away. This book enhances this sense of esteem in your heart, and gives revolutionary insight on what it means to maintain a Paradise mindset in this beautiful yet, interesting world.

Series 1: Paradise State of Mind

Overcoming Hardships in Life

Sometimes in life, hardships bring you closer to the Only Source of Healing. When you're stuck and you have nowhere else to go, and no one else to turn to it is Allah ﷻ that we call to. Hardships force us to realize our limitations, and to accept His Will. A great hardship in my own life, is what inspired me to write this book. I thought maybe, someone, somewhere out there in the world could one day benefit from the insight contained in this book. In the end, the goal is to know that you are truly not alone in what you face in this world, and that is the goal of this book. Within every human there are three components. The *ruuh (soul)*, the *nafs (soul+body)*, and the *jism (body)*. Knowing each part of yourself is essential to increasing the quality of your life, that way both your blessings and struggles in life will make sense to you. When you know who you are and where you come from, there is a sense of security and confidence you will maintain within you that no one can take away. If you are lost and you need directions, you need guidance. In this world we are uncertain, which means we are lost and in need of guidance. Allah ﷻ (swt) begins the Quran by the following verses:

"Alif. Laam. Meem"

"This is the Book about which there is no doubt, a guidance for those conscious of Allah" Quran 2:1-2

Every human on earth is lost, unless they have guidance. This means, we are born in a state of unawareness and we must search for our spiritual awareness. What wakes up our conscious, is knowing our reality. Those who look, and search will come to find that we are not alone in this world. That there is a being behind the very matter, atoms, molecules, and elements that make up this earth. He is the one who is holding the forces that make up nature together down to the tiniest particles. When you realize this, you will come to understand that this earth is a gift perfectly wrapped from Him to us. When someone gifts you something special, we should thank them. Allah (swt) says in the Quran:

"And if you were to count the blessings of Allah given to mankind, never will you be able to enumerate them. Surely Allah is indeed, Ever-Forgiving, Ever-Merciful"

Quran 16:18

Imagine if someone gave you a gift, and you took that gift used its blessings on everything else in the world but never thanked them? Your life is a gift, so will you not live this life to be thankful to the One who gave it to you? Your voice is a gift, will you use your voice to recite His words in a beautiful way, or use it on all the things that He dislikes? Your awareness is a gift, will you live up to your potential in seeking knowledge that will bring you closer to Him? Allah ﷻ says in the Quran:

"…Anyone who is grateful does so to the profit of his own soul…" (31:12)

Imagine, how blissful your inner consciousness can be when you live as a grateful servant to the Almighty. For example, when a *grateful servant* is thankful for the consciousness and mind that he was gifted by from Allah ﷻ, they will use every ounce of potential that they have to nurture this gift of intellect. When a *grateful servant* is thankful for the beautiful voice that they were gifted by from Allah ﷻ, they will not use that voice to profit

from singing or musical instruments...they will use that beautiful voice to recite His words from the Quran. When a *grateful servant*, is thankful for their wealth they will not waste it and indulge in worldly things that destroy their consciousness and morality. While many spend their wealth on name brand intoxicants, and ornamental objects of this world; a grateful servant will take that wealth and turn it into generational wealth for his future generations, and for the betterment of mankind. They will also take this wealth and use it to live an upright life that the *One who gifted them* loves. So, this is why when one is thankful it is a profit, an investment for their own soul - both in this life and in the next life.

Contemplating on this makes you realize two things; once a human realizes that they are lost in this world and begin to search for their purpose, they will come to know that there is a Creator. When they find out that this Creator is the one who gifted them life – a conscious soul will have no choice but to be grateful. This gratefulness does not add to the Kingdom of God, or take away from it. This gratefulness is actually an investment that a person makes for their own soul. Allah ﷻ says in the Quran:

"And remember when your proclaimed if you are thankful I will increase you in favor." Quran 14:7

The word gratitude is derived from the Latin word *gratia,* which means grace, graciousness, or gratefulness. In all realms of psychological research, gratitude is associated with more happiness. The reason why thankfulness, or gratitude is associated with happiness is because when people are thankful, they focus on what they have instead of what they lack.

Time is consistent and never stops for anyone. People who are consistently chasing the pleasures of life, forget the most essential component of life; that it does not last. They forget to live in the present moment, and focus on the reality that they are currently in. These kinds of people are people who live in the future, and this is what leads to anxiousness (anxiety). When a person is grateful, they see what they have in front of them. They feel the reality that they are experiencing in the current moment. Every interaction they have is meaningful, and when they are alone their mind is at ease because they are reminded of their blessings; from the very beat of their heart, to the rhythm of their steps.

They are more awake to the small pleasures of life. It is those who forgot the beauty that lies in the small pleasures, that constantly feel like something is missing. A grateful person has a higher chance of amplifying the quality of their life, because they live vicariously through the blessings they already have. Someone who is ungrateful, never gets out of this loop; the loop of constantly chasing what they do not have. Allah ﷻ says in the Quran:

"Competition in worldly increase diverts you, until you visit the graveyards. No, you are going to know, then no you are going to know. No, if you only knew with knowledge of certainty. That you will one day see the hell fire." Quran

It is a part of human nature to want to chase the finer things in life. A person who knows this aspect of their nature also knows its repercussions and they will do whatever they can to limit this part of their nature. Having a beautiful life and working towards worldly success is encouraged by our Created, but never at the expense of your own soul. One way you can limit this need for more and avoid the void that comes with the need for more, is by turning to Allāh.

Allah says in the Quran:

"So flee to Allah…" Quran

فقّرو إلى الله

So flee to Allah ﷻ,

from your lusts and desires,

from your past that haunts you down,

from the burdens of your heart,

from the evil of your soul,

from the future that you dread,

from your sins,

from the grief of your eyes.

Flee to Allah ﷻ, for you can only find refuge in Him.

Since time on earth is momentary, the pleasure that comes with success lasts for a brief moment as well. People tie their happiness into distant dreams, and once these dreams manifest and the moment is gone, they wonder why they are not happy. So, the only way to counteract this feeling of loss, is to chase the next big thing. It is a constant loop, and the chase for the next pleasure continues.

The human soul becomes stuck in a scavenger hunt for the elements of life; not realizing that the properties of these elements is not its cure. Within every human there are three components. The *ruuh (soul)*, the *nafs (soul+body)*, and the *jism (body)*. Knowing this, is essential to increase your quality of life. The soul and body are created from different material. What the body needs will not be the same as what the soul needs. Your body needs refreshment in the form of cleanliness, nutrition, and activity. Your soul needs refreshment in the form of spiritual consciousness, and connection to the source of life. Spiritual consciousness is the fundamental understanding that your body is a part of you, but your soul is the blueprint to your identity. Many in this world, have planted their main focus of betterment on their Nafs (ego), over their ruuh (spirit). A true believer in

Allah ﷻ, places a balanced focus on their Nafs (which is the body + soul), and their ruuh (spirit/soul).

Many things have been said about the Nafs in the Quran, but very little is known about the Ruuh (soul).

What we know about the Nafs (body) in the Quran:

The first way that the word *nafs* is expressed in the Quran, it is indicating our own-self. The self is composed of two parts the soul and the body. Right now, you are made up of your soul and your body. Your body is the encasing or the envelope for your soul.

Scholars use the terms *body* and *soul* to translate to the word nafs – interchangeably. This is because the Nafs is the entire being (the body + soul). Some people would translate it in English as self, some people would translate it in English as soul. The bottom line is, the nafs, is the soul and body connected together. An example of this is when Allah ﷻ Almighty says in the *Quran*:

وَاذْكُرْ رَبّكَ فِي نَفْسِكَ

And remember your Rabb inside your-self

[7:205]

The Three Types of Nafs (Self)

There are three types of *Nafs* in this world. Meaning, people are categorized as three:

1. Nafs-ul-ammarah

إِنَّ النَّفْسَ لَأَمَّارَةٌ بِالسُّوءِ

Indeed, the nafs that overwhelmingly commands a person

to do sin. [12:53]

This Nafsa (al-ammarah), is one that is ruling over the self. It commands over the soul, and takes over by fulfilling all carnal and worldly desires. A person who is in this position caters to their worldly body and its needs so much so, that they forget about their spirit. This means when the nafs has any desire, wish, or appetite, it simply commands that this desire be fulfilled.

In a sense this nafs, has sovereignty over the person. There is a form of subjugation that takes place, in which the soul is given less attention, and the worldly body is at the forefront of all attainment. A person who is in this category, often finds that they cater to their *nafs* (body) in every sense, even at the expense of their own spiritual and physical health.

If it is *ammarah* (guiding it to sin) this means a person is subordinate to it. It is guiding a person to misguidance. A sign that a person has this type of *nafs,* is that they sin blatantly and remorselessly. They do not have discipline over their nafs, so that they can guide it to what is best for them.

2. Nafs-ul-lawwamah

Lawwam means to self-incriminate. It is described as the self-reproaching person. This person is one who (unlike nafs-ul-ammara), is consciously aware of their deeds. So, when they sin they feel regret, and the express a sort of blame over themselves for the wrong that they have committed against themselves, or their Creator. A sign of a person who is in this category is one who commits a sin and feels remorse right after. They feel embarrassed and wish they could do better and take it back. These people often live their lives fighting a battle with their nafs, in which they commit sins and return to their Creator. Allah ﷻ calls them lawwamah – the *nafs* that checks

themselves before they wreck themselves. So, they fight this battle with their *nafs*, they try their best to direct it to do good and sometimes they fall short but when they do they always return to their Source (Allah ﷻ).

3. Nafs-ul-mutma'ina

يَا أَيَّتُهَا النَّفْسُ الْمُطْمَئِنَّةُ ارْجِعِي إِلَى رَبِّكِ رَاضِيَةً مَرْضِيَّةً

To the righteous it will be said "oh reassured soul, return

to your Lord well pleased, and pleasing to Him"

[89:27-28]

Here Allāh (God) address the *nafs* or person who is content. He

says, *mut'ma'ina*: oh, *reassured* one. This person is one who is

content with the hukm (wisdom) of Allah ﷻ, this nafs (soul and

body) has control over their soul, and body. They seamlessly

direct their *self* to what is good for them, and avoid the things

that are bad for them through discipline. Even if a thing looks

good or convenient for them at the moment like cheating,

stealing, serving their ego, or treating time as a luxury. They reassess their behavior and think of how it will serve them better in this life or in the next life. This person has molded and disciplined their worldly body (mind + heart), to achieve what is good for their soul. Their spirit is in line with what Allāh ﷻ loves for them, and that is prayer, that is love for their fellow humans, fulfilling the rights over their body and the rights others have over them.

This nafs (person or self), is one who reached a state of inner peace, and serenity within themselves. This of course means they feel peace within themselves, that they have achieved the ability to control their desires. They have achieved the ability to not want the things that they (once wanted), that are not good for them or no longer serves them. Their *nafs* has become so used to valuing the things that Allāh ﷻ loves, and disregarding the things that He does not love.

So, these are the three types of nafs. Nafs-ul-Ammarah, Nafs-ul-Lawwamah and Nafs-ul-Mutmainnah.

I am guessing by now that you have already seen bits and pieces of yourself in either of the three categories. Now, it is up to you to do what it takes to enrich your soul with all that it needs to direct itself towards success in this life and in the next.

Remember, we will achieve the highest elevation for our *nafs* by correcting and improving its state. How can this be done? Allah ﷻ says in the Quran:

أَنْفُسَكُمْ عَلَيْكُمْ آمَنُوا الَّذِينَ أَيُّهَا يَا

"O you who have believed, upon you is [responsibility for] yourselves." Quran 5:105

In exact translation, Allah ﷻ says – "oh you who believe it is upon yourselves…"

مَنْ يَضُرُّكُمْ لَا اهْتَدَيْتُمْ إِذَا ضَلَّ جَمِيعًا مَرْجِعُكُمْ اللَّهِ إِلَى

تَعْمَلُونَ كُنْتُمْ بِمَا فَيُنَبِّئُكُمْ

"…that you are responsible over your *self*. Anyone who is

misguided cannot harm you if you are guided, one day you will return to your Creator, and He will tell of all you used to do."

We can achieve elevation for our *nafs* by knowing the responsibility we have over it. We can do this by being reminded that one day, we will return to our Creator, stand before Him, and He will tell us of all that we used to do on earth. Knowing this will help us be more conscious of our time, and what we feed our souls.

Meeting Allah ﷻ 5x a Day

You want to know what true success is? Spending every minute, immersing yourself in the moment. People think success is a destination that lives in the future. Success is what you choose to do right now. This is what Allah ﷻ tells us. Success is an experience you have 5 times a day, when you have the chance to stand before Allah ﷻ in your prayers. You meet Allah ﷻ (God) 5 times a day in prayer, and will meet him Jannah (paradise). You can create a paradise in your heart by immersing yourself in the prayer. You are indeed standing before Allah, when you pray. The moment you raised your hands and say "Allahu Akbar" (God is the Greatest), and begin prayer, you are attesting that Allah ﷻ is bigger than all of your problems and worries.

This is why praying 5 times a day is a part of success.

Many people think that ultimate success is in their careers – where they work under a boss, earning a salary that they will one day leave on this earth. Success is the currency that you earn through the good deeds you do, through your prayer, through charity work, through the knowledge you leave behind for the people on earth.

All of these things are valuable, because their impact is something that will last when you leave this earth. Money, and material goods will not follow you to the grave. The only thing that you will take with you is the light you developed within your soul.

The most successful people are the ones who realize this. The ones who envelope their time around the prayers, knowing that it is the main success they experience every day. They also know that these very prayers are what they have prepared for the meeting with their Lord. Imagine this, you have a long-lost friend who has gifted you with every single thing that you own in life, including a check of $100,000. All this friend asks is that you remember to thank him throughout the day in return. How would it feel for your friend if you forgot to thank him for the favors he's done for you?

Let's say you meet up with this friend again one day, and face them after being ungrateful to them. It would surely feel embarrassing, knowing that you forgot all about them but they were the ones giving you monthly checks to live your best life.

Allah ﷻ gave us a life, our soul, our hearts and minds. None of it belongs to us. All of it belongs to him. We are renting, and he is the sole owner. So, imagine how there are people who pass on to the next life, who have not built a connection with their Creator; or don't even know who He is. This is why the most successful person is the one who befriends Allah ﷻ here on earth, before finally meeting Him on the Day of Judgement.

There are people in this world who converse with Allah ﷻ as if He is their own best friend. They know in the depth of their hearts that he knows them better than they know themselves. So, they trust that no one else on earth can understand them better. These are the people who stay up at night, while the rest of the world sleeps, the people reconnect with their Originator and the Originator of all things.

Allah ﷻ says of them in the Quran:

1.   "O you wrapped in garments (i.e. Prophet Muhammad)!

2. Stand (to pray) all night, except a little —

3. Half of it or a little less than that,

4. Or a little more. And recite the Qur'an (aloud) in a slow, (pleasant tone and) style.

5. Verily, We shall send down to you a weighty Word (i.e. obligations, laws).

6. Verily, the rising by night (for Tahajjud prayer) is very hard and most potent and good for governing oneself, and most suitable for (understanding) the Word (of Allaah)"

Virtue of Tahajjud for the Soul

Why is it that tahajjud (praying during the night), is considered a virtue loved by Allah? The reason is because people do what they love most during the late hours of the night. When do people celebrate their weddings? During the day, or at night?

When do people enjoy partying? During the day or during the night? All of the events that bring people together usually happen late at night. We take solace in the peace that the darkness of the night brings. So, people who spend their time in prayer at night, are the most loved by their Creator (Allāh ﷻ).

So long as you continue to turn back to Him, so long as you realize He is a forgiving Lord, know that Allah ﷻ will forgive you no matter what you have done.

How to pray Tahajjud (Night Prayers)

There is a quote that I love,

"you defeat Satan with patience, he is very patient, so you should be even more patient."

Discipline your nafs to enjoy prayers at night, and organize and manage your time in a way that allows you to take advantage of your time; this is so important!

I went through a phase in my own life, where I thought that the extra prayers, the qiyam, the tahajjud, and the Sunnah prayers were just there as options for the elders. In my mind, I thought that praying the bare minimum was good enough. Then one day, I remember waking up specifically for work at 4:30 a.m. in the morning. I made sure that I got that morning shower in, I made sure that I had a good breakfast by 5:30 a.m. so that I can have the proper energy while at work, and I had my clothes laid out ready to wear. Then I thought to myself, I do all of this work. I go to work for a company, under a boss, and my manager – and I put this extra preparation early in the morning for work. How come I don't put in the same preparation for my eternity? The prophet Mohamed (peace be upon him) said;

"The two Rak'ah **before** the dawn

(Fajr) prayer are **better than** this **world** and all it

contains." [Muslim]

That's when it hit me, I truly need to find the correct balance in my life so that I can take advantage of my time here on earth. I honestly don't want to go to the day of judgement, standing before God, and having done the bare minimum in my worship to Him. If I could put all of that preparation in the work I do for humans on earth, why can I not prepare for my prayers with that same energy and more?

This is why, in this book, I want to teach you and outline to you how to pray Tahajjud prayers so that you too, can build a life where your heart finds peace in the night prayers. It's truly a beautiful thing, when (as a millennial in this wild generation) you find the perfect balance in your life to incorporate God. The world we live in today is completely trying to take God out of the equation; whether it is through science, informational outlets, or entertainment industries. To be able to overcome all of these influences and seamlessly make connecting with Allah ﷻ apart of your daily routine is a blessing and a gift.

Tahajjud Prayers

Conditions of offering Tahajjud Prayer

1. Make an intention of performing Tahajjud prayer and rearrange to wake up finally a piece of the night.

2. Make sure to perform Wudu as one should perform before every tahajjud

3. Move to a clean and quiet place in the house being away from distractions.

4. Offer at least two Raka`ts up to 12, depending on one`s willpower.

5. Don't forget to supplicate to Allah SWT for one`s just and rightful requests in order to get benefited from this exceedingly rewarding hour of darkness.

The maximum is 12 raka'at . The minimum is 2.

An example of Tahajjud broken down

2 raka'a (unit)

2 raka'a (unit)

2 raka'a (unit)

2 raka'a (unit)

2 raka'a (unit)

2 raka'a (unit)

Then after praying up to a total of 12 raka'at (units), you must add one raka'a of Witr, so that your prayer can become an odd number.

During each unit recite your favorite surahs, or even learn specific surahs during the day, so that you can recite them at night as well. Remember this is the time you are dedicating to your Creator and a currency that you are collecting for your hereafter. The currency of this world is money, but the currency of the next world will be your good deeds. The best judgement that we can give and make right now, is the one that we do over ourselves. The companions of the prophet Mohamed often remembered the next world, and did so by judging their deeds here on earth before their meeting with Allah ﷻ. One way that helps is by recording all the good and bad you have done in your own book of records.

Benefits of Tahajjud prayer

- It gives inner strength
- It gives you mental endurance
- A chance to get closer to the Creator
- A chance to earn His mercy & forgiveness

- The doors of Mercy and Forgiveness are open during the last 1/3 of night
- There is an hour during that night where prayers are accepted so it is the best time to ask
- It is a huge incentive for the believer to wake up when everyone else is asleep and remember Allah (SWT) alone
- Tahajjud prayer can strengthen religious understanding
- It can bring fresh inspiration and insight on your life and the world
- Tahajjud prayer can prevent wickedness and prevent acts of sin
- Tahajjud prayer can strengthen your memory and give you profound judgement on life tests and trials

Keeping a Book of Records

This is an idea that I have thought of recently, but I am sure it is not one that is unique. There has to be people out there who do this. However, this idea is keeping your own special notebook where you record your good and bad deeds; so that you are conscious and aware of all that you have done for yourself during the day. That way when you make duaa, you know exactly what you should ask forgiveness for and you also have an idea on the things you can improve on. Maybe you find that you delay prayers, and it is something that you should put more emphasis on or maybe you find that you procrastinate your meetings with people. Whatever it may be, you have an idea of what you could do to improve. Also keeping this notebook is a reminder to you, that there is a real book that the angels have. They are currently busy writing all of your deeds. Whenever you are about to commit a wrong action you will remember that you have to write it in your notebook. It will be a sole reminder to you of the book that Allah ﷻ will give you on the Day of Judgement.

<u>Truly your success is in prayer</u>

I was once told by my sheikh whose name is Ustadh – Abduldahir (who I memorized the Quran from), he told me that "…no matter what you do in life stick to your prayers. As long as you pray your daily prayers, you will be successful in everything you commit to in your life. Remain steadfast with your prayers, and you will see that everything else will follow through." I never forgot that advise, and it was always in line with what my parents also advised me about the prayers.

We know that we should pray, but do we actually try to understand the benefits? I realized when I started taking my prayers more seriously, and actually planned my day around the prayers, my mindset was slowly revolutionizing. Prayers require punctuality, it requires that you be on time, and it requires focus. When you are going about your daily life, you are so focused on catering to your body and mind, and your soul becomes neglected. This neglect, causes you to put more emphasis on your worldly success and forget about your eternal success. The five daily prayers, allow you to pause midway through this chaos of life, and refocus your attention on God and your meeting with Him in the next world. It puts into perspective that while you work for your worldly success, there is a greater success that is calling you, and that matters more. This is the success you will receive when you are gifted your eternity in heaven.

A lot of people message me on Instagram about the prayers, and what they can do to better their punctuality, or even find it in themselves to pray. I would advise that you remember Allah ﷻ as much as you can first. You cannot pray during the day, if you are forgetful of Allah ﷻ. Teaching your mind to be reminded of the blessings you have right now, and how all of it is from Him, should make you shy to miss your meeting with Him.

Also, be reminded of how there are people right now, who are your age that are taking full advantage of their youth and connecting with God. There should be a sense of urgency, or even jealousy that Allah ﷻ could love someone else and you are *just there*, focusing on things that won't bring you benefit. You know what I mean?

Let me tell you a quick story, and this is a true story. Perhaps this story will bring to light the reality of this world, that you may have overlooked. This is the story of a revert sister named Amy Klooz and she narrates:

When I embraced Islam, my biggest challenge was learning to pray. Of course, I had "prayed" before, as a Christian, but in Islam prayer means more–it is a ritual of submission involving body and mind. I wanted to pray, but like everything else, I didn't know how to start, and so I spent my first 6 months after my *shahadah* not practicing at all. After a bad experience at a masjid, I wanted nothing to do with the local Muslim community.

I knew I should learn to pray, probably start wearing a scarf, maybe learn Arabic, and even fast when Ramadan came around. And at times, I really tried. I had a book on how to perform *salah*, but for some reason whenever I would stand up to try, it all seemed completely incomprehensible.

After trying to sound out the Arabic transliterated in my book, I felt so desperate and overwhelmed that I just put my face on the floor and cried. From the depths of my heart I begged to learn how to pray so I could follow the Quran, and finally establish prayers in my life.

It didn't happen overnight. But before long I reached out to the mosque again, asking specifically for someone to show me how to pray. Eventually I heard back from a lady who asked me to meet her before the Friday prayers. There, she gave me a quick overview of how to perform a 2-rak'ah prayer.

The only things I could memorize then were *"Allahu Akbar"* and the two repeated supplications, *"Subhaana Rabbiy al-Adheem"* while bowing, and *"Subhaana Rabbiy al-A'laa"* while prostrating. But after the sermon I followed along in the prayer; and even though I didn't understand anything else, I had actually, prayed *salah* for the first time.

After that, things started changing for me, and fast. When I got home, I tried diligently to not miss any prayers, and if I forgot one or overslept then I made it up right away. And since I couldn't pray with a group all the time, I made myself a "cheat sheet" with the transliterated Arabic on one side and the English on the other. First, I read the English during prayers, only using the Arabic phrases I already knew. But before long, I had the

English memorized. So I started reading the Arabic, until I had that memorized too.

In just a couple of weeks I was reading the entire prayer from memory in Arabic (albeit heavily accented) and I knew what each part meant. And once I started praying, as I was forming a relationship with Allah by means of daily prayer, my life started to change. Committing to *salah* changed my schedule, my wardrobe, my relationship with the community, and my relationship with the Quran.

How Praying Changed My Schedule

The first change I noticed was in my daily schedule–I had to get up earlier, in time to pray the morning (*fajr*) prayer. That meant I also had to get to bed earlier. I had to find places to pray at school, and at work, and I even arranged my course schedule so I could attend Friday prayers. When Ramadan came, I was diligent about finding time to study so I could still attend night prayers. While the time-blocking could have made me more stressed out, it actually made me more productive. That shouldn't be surprising, given this *hadith*: The Prophet (peace be upon him) said:

"O Allah, bless my people in their early mornings." (Abu Dawud)

How Praying Changed My Wardrobe

The next big change for me was to start wearing hijab. I didn't start immediately–at first I would only put it on to pray. But I also needed to be sure my clothes covered the rest of me. Soon I started wearing the scarf to the mosque, putting it on while riding the bus, for instance. Eventually I would leave it on for longer periods of time afterwards, occasionally during class or while out shopping. After a few weeks of wearing it sometimes, I started wearing it full-time.

The most drastic aspect of this change, however, was that before starting to pray, I had absolutely no desire whatsoever to wear hijab. And within a month or two it had become not just convenient but also comfortable.

How Praying Gave Me Community

A third major change when I started praying was becoming part of the Muslim community. By wearing a scarf, I met other Muslims on campus. By attending Friday prayers, I started to meet other Muslims at the mosque. I started attending educational programs, and when my parents kicked me out, through the mosque I found a Muslim roommate. The five daily prayers are a kind of glue that holds the Muslim community together–at first it just gave me a reason to socialize with other Muslims, though eventually they became some of my closest friends.

How Praying Taught Me Quran

One more major change I noticed after praying was that I wanted to learn more Quran. Reading the same *surah* time after time began to feel less satisfying, knowing there are over 600 more pages to be memorize and recite.

Prayer gave me my first motivation to learn to read Arabic, and to start memorizing Quran–plus daily opportunities to review what I had already memorized. That eventually led me to study Arabic more deeply when the opportunities arose.

Alhamdulillah, reading the Quran in Arabic, with comprehension, and memorizing it, are now all part of my daily routine. And daily prayers are still a motivation to keep learning, to improve my prayers.

Conclusion

The Quran says:

{We have not sent down to you the Quran that you be distressed.} (20:02)

Unfortunately, I was distressed when I began my journey as a

Muslim, but once daily prayer became part of my routine, my life changed for the better.

Establishing prayer and making it part of your daily routine, can change your life too, *Insha'Allah*.

(end quote)

As you can see, prayers truly revolutionize your life. I am sure you here this all the time, but it is true. Remember, we learned that food is nourishment for your body. Now, you know that praying is soul-food for your spirit.

On earth, you will see many people unhappy with their lives, and those are people who are successful in their worldly pursuits. They have millions of dollars, cars, houses in different locations, and even a social network of people that they can use to their advantage. Still, there is a void. There is something that is missing in their hearts and they can't put their hands on it. So they live their life in search of a way to fill this void. They think maybe I need new friends, they find great friends and still something is missing. They think maybe, I should go out and party a little more I am always in the house; they go out and the pleasure is momentary. They are back in their homes wondering to themselves what is it that I am missing, why do I feel this way. Then they think, maybe I need to take advantage of this fame that I have, and still they feel alone. They come to the realization maybe if I had a partner, I will feel happy again, then I won't be lonely, and this void I feel inside will be gone. So, they find themselves someone they see fit for their companionship, and when the pleasure of that chase is over they are back at square one.

Why is it that a person can have the whole world to their disposal and still feel empty inside? It is because their bodies have had its fill of worldly success but their soul is bare and empty like a desert. They have starved their soul of what it needs to connect to Godliness, and it is enveloped in a dark place waiting to be watered with the remembrance of Allah ﷻ.

Still, they are unaware and so they walk the earth w ith an exterior that boasts of success, but their insides are barren and in need of rain.

Then there are some in this world, who live out in the open. They are in open communities, who serve and help one another, while they live in bare minimum conditions. You see that their exterior condition is filled with daily struggles. Yet, they have smiles on their faces, and a hope inside of them that illuminates their entire visage. They live with very few material goods and yet their hearts are filled with contentment. These are people who, even though they lack worldly success, their soul is filled with spiritual success. Paradise is in their hearts, and so every hardship they face is presented to them as a momentary trial. They face the storm with conviction that it is a reality that Allah ﷻ will allow them to overcome.

These are the people that we should learn from, live among so that we can gain the spiritual insight that they have gained through their hardships.

Imagine this, someone who is given this entire world and they never face an ounce of hardship. Compare this person to one who has faced hardships in life, and has overcome them. They are not in the same position in life. One is lacking spiritual insight, and another graduated in their intellect and worldly insight. So never once belittle your hardships in life, try to find the lessons in them, so that you can learn from them.

You are meant to go through obstacles in life so that you can teach your future children how they can overcome, and learn from the lessons that you had to learn the hard way. You are meant to face hardships so that they bring you back to Allah ﷻ, and make you further away from the Shaytan (Satan) who wants you to go to hell for eternity.

In order to evolve in your spirituality, and change the course of your life for the better, it is important for you to know who Allah ﷻ is. The very first verses that were revealed in the Quran were not about prayers, hajj, charity, or praying tahajjud during the night. The first verses that God revealed to mankind, was so that mankind can know who He is. If you were to receive an unknown letter from someone and they didn't tell you who they were, you wouldn't trust that letter. You would not have understanding of the person behind that letter and what their agenda is. So, Allāh ﷻ wants you to know who He is. Many

verses in the Quran are God (Allāh ﷻ), explaining His

characteristics and attributes. Since we cannot see Allāh ﷻ, and

do not have the mental capacity to do so. Allāh ﷻ often points

to the creation that He has created such as the sun, the moon, and the stars – so that we may take heed of how great His artistry and ability is. The magnitude of the heavens itself is a description that God (Allāh ﷻ) uses to describe His power and

greatness. His Greatness is termed as "Allahu-Akbar" which

means *God is Great*. This term unfortunately, is widely

misunderstood as a call for violence when in reality it simply

expresses the Greatness of the One who created us.

As we read through the Quran, we notice that Allāh ﷻ

expresses Himself through His 99 names or attributes. This does

not mean that there is more than One God. They are simply

names that describe His personality, and Divine characteristics.

Before we get to those names, let us first learn about Allāh and

who He is.

Who is Allah ﷻ?

God took for himself the name" Allah" ﷻ. The name Allah ﷻ

is neither masculine nor feminine. Rather, He is incomparable to

any living creature He created. While most Christians I know

may argue "God created us in his image." Muslims believe God

is nothing like his creation. He is unable to be perceived by any

of the senses, since we have no knowledge of the unseen.

Among the names He chose for himself includes, the most powerful and the all-knowing; the giver and the taker; the wise and the generous; while He is the most merciful to his creation, He can also be stern in punishment if needed.

His attributes and names that are used to praise Him are 99. To name a few; the Almighty, the Majestic, the Creator, the Forgiver, the Honorable and the Guardian of his creation. Last but not least in the following verse, God describes Himself in great detail "Allah! There is no god but He – the Living, The Self-Subsisting, Eternal. No slumber can seize Him nor sleep. His are all things In the heavens and on earth. Who is there that can intercede In His presence except as He permits? He knows what appears to His creatures before, after or behind them. Nor shall they compass any of his knowledge except as He wills. His throne extends Over the heavens and on earth, and He never feels fatigue in guarding And preserving them, for He is the Most High. The Supreme in glory." [Surah al-Baqarah 2: 255]

And what is more better than worshiping God, the way he deserves?

Before I mentioned the characteristics of God in Islam. His 99 names were revealed to the prophet Mohamed (peace be upon him), and many prophets before that were familiar with his most sublime names. In the English language, Gods name can take many forms. It can become plural like 'gods' or 'goddesses'. However, the name God took for himself 'Allah' ﷻ cannot be made into a plural form. This indicates that he is unique and no being can reach his status.

"Say (O Mohamed), 'He is Allah, the One;

Allah, the Eternal, Absolute;

He begets not, and neither is He begotten;

And there is nothing that can be compared to Him."

Qur'an 112:1-4

Gods power can be seen through his creation. In fact, the last prophet; Mohamed (peace be upon him) encourages Muslims to know themselves in order to know Allah ﷻ. One should look at the way they were created. God gave us eyes to see, a mouth to speak, hands to use, and feet to be able to walk around. Most importantly he gave us intellect and a mind so that we may reason and use logic. All of these are countless blessings that he is showering us with and in return what do human beings do? We constantly take his words as a jest. We don't realize that this life is only temporary and there is a greater meaning as to why we are here.

"Do the people think that they will be left to say, "We believe" and they will not be tried?" 29:2

In the holy Qur'an God encourages human beings in countless verses to use logic and reason, to find out who He is. An example of that would be the verse;

"It is a Book We have sent down to you, full of blessing, so let people of intelligence ponder (liyaddabbaru) its Signs and take heed." [38:29]

"Will they not then ponder the Qur'an or are there locks

upon their hearts?" [Muhammad, 47:24]

In order to understand God, the correct way one must open the Qur'an and read it. One day I was with young children I teach on Saturday's. One of them asked me a really great question. She said, "How is that a person can die right now where we live and that same second another person is taking their last breath in another part of the world? How does the Angel of Death work so fast?" I told her, "If Allah ﷻ can cause us to speak, think and

contemplate without any problems; and at the other side of the world people are speaking, thinking and contemplating as we are now; What makes you think he can't take the souls of people simultaneously at the same time?"

These names are the realities of Allah ﷻ. They are the

characteristics of the most Beautiful Being, the Loving, Compassionate, Sovereign, most Powerful, most Merciful. These names of Allah ﷻ are not the only names of Allah. These

are only the names known and revealed to mankind through the Quran. In fact there are many more beautiful characteristics not known to mankind. Some that we don't know are known by the Angels, the previous Prophets and Messengers and to certain men of God who are beloved by the most High due to their deeds. The Divine Nature of Allah ﷻ is infinite, and

unimaginable. Your Lord is the Originator of the heavens, the earth, and all that is in between. And He is also the Originator of Love. Love begins with Him, continues through Him, and eternally exists by Him. Love your Creator enough to forbid what He doesn't Love, and Allah ﷻ will bestow upon you love.

Perhaps that love that Allah ﷻ envelopes around your entire

being, will cause you to love yourself. This love you gain for

yourself will then manifest itself around you and spread. Love

Allah and Allah will love you.

"Say, to them, O Muhammad, 'If you love Allah, then follow

me, Allah will love you, and forgive you your sins.' Allah is

Forgiving, most Merciful." Quran 3:31

This is what Islam teaches. Islam teaches, that the One who

Created us does not live for a specified time, rather He is eternal.

The Lord does not possess any human weaknesses. The One

who gives life and death, has never been deprived of existence,

and will continue to exist. The One who gives rest, has never fell

into the influence of sleep or slumber. Sleep is a state of

unawareness, the Almighty is the All-Aware, and Ever-Aware.

Sleep is a gift that the Creator bestowed upon mankind. To ever

say that the Creator of this universe is in need of rest, will mean

that this entire universe will fall off course. This universe is in

need of Allah ﷻ, this universe is in need of the Awareness of its

Creator.

"no sleep overtakes Him, nor slumber..." Quran 2:255

The orbit, the sun, the moon; indeed, the most-High ﷻ is in

control of all of these realities. In order for everything in

existence to stay on course it would require proper awareness.

Thus, Allah ﷻ is also the Maintainer and Sustainer of this

universe. The creation of this world, does not have the capabilities to sustain and maintain itself. As humans, we are not in control of the properties in the atmosphere that cooperate with the functions of our lungs, or the vessels in our blood that are responsible for the beat of our hearts. All of these realities must have an Originator, One who is responsible for its function.

"He is the Originator of all that is in the heavens and the earth..." Quran

The Almighty Lord, is the most Merciful. The Mercy of Allah ﷻ can be seen in the Creation of the night and the day. Mankind finds in vast heavens the brilliant sun, its radiant magnanimity and wide scope which covers the entire heavens, useful for their daily endeavors. The absence of the suns brilliance is replaced with darkness. Conveniently mankind looks to the sky once again and finds a radiant lamp giving light and heavens furthermore filled with stars. The lamp serving as a light in the darkness, and the stars positioned in accuracy used as a guiding compass by men. Everything in this universe is created by the Lord and enveloped with His Everlasting Compassion and Mercy. The mercy of Allah ﷻ can be seen in his messages and revelation to mankind. The Mercy of Allah can be seen in every aspect of the creation, to name each and every circumstance in this universe that exhibits signs of the Merciful nature of the most-High ﷻ will fill entire volumes, and books endlessly.

Understanding Energy

Energy is simultaneous, and it continues on endlessly. It can neither be created nor destroyed. Energy is real in all its forms, and it has a major effect on our bodies and souls. The whole universe is made up of energy. This energy is expressed through different vibrations (vibes), and frequencies. Your thoughts and your energy will attract the kind of world in which you live.

The whole universe is made up of energy and vibrations. Every thought that you have has a certain wavelength. For example, "I want pizza right now" has a different wavelength than, "I have to clean the house," your energy changes after each thought, while you are unaware.

We know that energy can neither be created nor destroyed and that it is from Allah ﷻ. What you give in this world is what you get. The world around us is far beyond the compact mass we see with our naked eyes. And we, human beings, are far beyond the compact mass of flesh and bones that we recognize and see. We are swimming in a vast sea of energy.

Thoughts become ideas, and ideas become actions. Thoughts, ideas, and actions are all forms of energy. Since the world is made up of energy, it makes sense that this energy can be translated in a specific universal law. Best explanation:

Ice (solid) – water (liquid) – vapor (gas)

They change under certain energy pressures

If objects can change due to energy, what do you think about the energy

that comes from your mind and your heart?

We send and receive energy continuously each second of our life; or in other words we gain or lose energy from and to our surroundings each second of our life. So, if energy cannot be destroyed or created then it makes sense that whatever action we energize into this universe is recorded and it will return to you in the same exact form. Whether you receive the good that you did in this life, or in the next depends. But you will always gain the good energy that you put forth back in your life, and the bad that you put forth back in your life. Allah tells us in the Quran:

"So, whoever does an atom's weight of good will see it, and whoever does an atoms weight of evil shall see it."

Quran 99:7-8

This verse shows us that whatever energy you put forth will not disappear, it will come back to you in some form whether it is in this life or in the next life.

Furthermore, since the whole world is made up of energy, take heed of those moments that you feel someone else's energy. You can often feel their energy, without them intending you to know. You can feel is what someone intends for you is good or bad at times based on their demeanor and body language, it's really their energy translating into vibrations. You should learn to trust this feeling (at times), because people's bad energy can affect you. That is why prophet Muhammad emphasized surrounding yourself around good companionship, and those who are seeking to direct themselves towards Allāh ﷻ. These are the people who are the most genuine because their only concern is making sure their connection with Allāh ﷻ is on point. They will not envy you, because they know their blessing and qadr (destiny) is with Allāh ﷻ. They will not have any vendetta or silent resentment against you because they truly feel a genuine care for all of Allāh's ﷻ creation. When they see the reality of this world and what it means, they will speak words that will allow one to increase in iman and insight.

Knowing the names of Allah ﷻ is important, and repeating His names is important for your own energy. It helps you remember the beauty of the One who created you, and His magnitude.

Imagine, when you say His names – you are speaking the names of the one who is responsible for creating this entire universe. The prophet Muhammad said of Al-Asma-ul-Husna (الحُسناى آلاسْمَاءُ) – the most beautiful names of Allāh:

Narrated Abu Huraira: Prophet Muhammad SAW said, "Allah has ninety-nine names, i.e. one-hundred minus one, and whoever knows them will go to Paradise."

Sahih Al-Bukhari – Book 50 Hadith 894

An-Nawawi said, "To preserve them is said to mean to enumerate and count them in one's supplication by them. It is said it means to persevere in them, to respect them in the best manner, to guard what they require, and to affirm their meanings. And it is said the meaning is to act by them and to obey Allah ﷻ according to the implications of every name."

Throughout the day, find ways to connect the sights that you see with the names of Allah. Find ways to connect His names through the lessons you learn in life as well, because the best person is truly the one who can see the world through Him.

Allāh ﷻ says in a Hadith Qudsi (which is a form of hadith in which the prophet spoke what Allāh said to Him directly):

"My servant draws not near to Me with anything more loved by Me than the religious duties I have enjoined upon him, and My servant continues to draw near to Me with supererogatory works so that I shall love him. When I love him, I am his hearing with which he hears, his seeing with which he sees, his hand with which he strikes and his foot with which he walks. Were he to ask [something] of Me, I would surely give it to him, and were he to ask Me for refuge, I would surely grant him it. I do not hesitate about anything as much as I hesitate about [seizing] the soul of My faithful servant: he hates death and I hate hurting him." (Hadith Bukhari)

The following list consists of the most common and agreed-upon names of Allah ﷻ, which were explicitly found in the Quran or Hadith:

- **Allah** - *The single, proper name for God in Islam*

- **Ar-Rahman** - *The Compassionate, The Beneficent*

- **Ar-Raheem** - *The Merciful*

- **Al-Malik** - *The King, The Sovereign Lord*

- **Al-Quddoos** - *The Holy*

- **As-Salaam** - *The Source of Peace*

- **Al-Mu'min** - *The Guardian of Faith*

- **Al-Muhaimin** - *The Protector*

- **Al-'Aziz** - *The Mighty, The Strong*

- **Al-Jabbaar** - *The Compeller*

- **Al-Mutakabbir** - *The Majestic*

- **Al-Khaaliq** - *The Creator*

- **Al-Bari'** - *The Evolver, The Maker*

- **Al-Musawwir** - *The Fashioner*

- **Al-Ghaffaar** - *The Great Forgiver*

- **Al-Qahhaar** - *The Subduer, The Dominant*

- **Al-Wahhaab** - *The Bestower*

- **Al-Razzaaq** - *The Sustainer, The Provider*

- **Al-Fattaah** - *The Opener, The Reliever*

- **Al-'Aleem** - *The All-Knowing*

- **Al-Qaabid** - *The Retainer*

- **Al-Baasit** - *The Expander*

- **Al-Khaafid** - *The Abaser*

- **Al-Raafi'** - *The Exalter*

- **Al-Mu'iz** - *The Honorer*

- **Al-Muthil** - *The Humiliator*

- **As-Samee'** - *The All-Hearing*

- **Al-Baseer** - *The All-Seeing*

- **Al-Hakam** - *The Judge*

- **Al-'Adl** - *The Just*

- **Al-Lateef** - *The Subtle One*

- **Al-Khabeer** - *The Aware*

- **Al-Haleem** - *The Forebearing*

- **Al-'Azeem** - *The Great One*

- **Al-Ghafoor** - *The All-Forgiving*

- **Ash-Shakoor** - *The Grateful*

- **Al-'Aliyy** - *The Most High*

- **Al-Kabeer** - *The Great*

- **Al-Hafeez** - *The Preserver*

- **Al-Muqeet** - *The Maintainer*

- **Al-Haseeb** - *The Reckoner*

- **Al-Jaleel** - *The Sublime One*

- **Al-Kareem** - *The Generous*

- **Ar-Raqeeb** - *The Watcher*

- **Al-Mujeeb** - *The Responsive*

- **Al-Wasi'** - *The Vast*

- **Al-Hakeem** - *The Wise*

- **Al-Wadood** - *The Loving*

- **Al-Majeed** - *The Glorious*

- **Al-Ba'ith** - *The Resurrector*

- **Ash-Shaheed** - *The Witness*

- **Al-Haqq** - *The Truth*

- **Al-Wakeel** - *The Trustee*

- **Al-Qawiyy** - *The Strong*

- **Al-Mateen** - *The Firm One*

- **Al-Waliyy** - *The Supporter*

- **Al-Hameed** - *The Praiseworthy*

- **Al-Muhsee** - *The Counter*

- **Al-Mubdi'** - *The Originator*

- **Al-Mu'eed** - *The Reproducer*

- **Al-Muhyi** - *The Restorer*

- **Al-Mumeet** - *The Destroyer*

- **Al-Hayy** - *The Alive*

- **Al-Qayyoom** - *The Self-Subsisting*

- **Al-Waajid** - *The Perceiver*

- **Al-Waahid** - *The Unique*

- **Al-Ahad** - *The One*

- **As-Samad** - *The Eternal*

- **Al-Qaadir** - *The Able*

- **Al-Muqtadir** - *The Powerful*

- **Al-Muqaddim** - *The Expediter*

- **Al-Mu'akh-khir** - *The Delayer*

- **Al-'Awwal** - *The First*

- **Al-'Akhir** - *The Last*

- **Az-Zaahir** - *The Manifest*

- **Al-Baatin** - *The Hidden*

- **Al-Walee** - *The Governor*

- **Al-Muta'ali** - *The Most Exalted*

- **Al-Barr** - *The Source of All Goodness*

- **At-Tawwaab** - *The Acceptor of Repentance*

- **Al-Muntaqim** - *The Avenger*

- **Al-'Afuww** - *The Pardoner*

- **Ar-Ra'uf** - *The Compassionate*

- **Malik Al-Mulk** - *The King of Kings*

- **Thul-Jalali wal-Ikram** - *The Lord of Majesty and Bounty*

- **Al-Muqsit** - *The Equitable*

- **Al-Jaami'** - *The Gatherer*

- **Al-Ghaniyy** - *The Self-Sufficient*

- **Al-Mughni** - *The Enricher*

- **Al-Maani'** - *The Preventer*

- **Ad-Daarr** - *The Distresser*

- **An-Nafi'** - *The Propitious*

- **An-Noor** - *The Light*

- **Al-Haadi** - *The Guide*

- **Al-Badi'** - *The Incomparable*

- **Al-Baaqi** - *The Everlasting*

- **Al-Waarith** - *The Inheritor*

- **Ar-Rasheed** - *The Guide to the Right Path*

- **As-Saboor** - *The Patient*

Importance of making mention of Allāh's name throughout the day

Allah ﷻ the Almighty said: "I am as My servant thinks I am

(1). I am with him when he makes mention of Me. If he makes mention of Me to himself, I make mention of him to Myself; and if he makes mention of Me in an assembly, I make mention of him in an assembly better than it. And if he draws near to Me an arm's length, I draw near to him a cubit, and if he draws near to Me a cubit, I draw near to him a fathom. And if he comes to Me walking, I go to him at speed." (Hadith Qudsi).

Imagine how Merciful our Creator is, one step towards Him and He rushes to our aid in full speed. I truly believe that making mention of Allāh's names and reflecting on them not only bring peace to your heart physically, but it also gives you a spiritual advantage in this life because of how close it brings you towards Allāh ﷻ.

How to Incorporate Allāh's names into your life

One way that you could internalize the names of Allāh ﷻ in your heart, is by reflecting on the nature surrounding you, reflecting on the lessons you learned from your hardships, and the reality of your own human nature.

The nature surrounding you is obviously filled with a lot of reflections of Allāh's ﷻ attributes. For example, when you look

at His creation, you know the He created them and that He is *Al-Khaliq* (the Creator), and *Al-Musawir* (the Designer). When you

look at the blessings that His creation receive on a daily basis,

you know that he is *Al-Qaadir* (the Able), and *Al-Kareem* (the

Generous). When you look to the magnitude of the sun, and how

big it is (that it can fit 1.3 million earths), you know that He is

Al-Qawiy (the most Strong). When you see the atmosphere and

how far the galaxy stretches and expands, you know that He is

Al-Aly (the most High).

These are all the ways that we can see the attributes, the blue

print of Allāhs ﷻ personality through the art that He has

created.

Another way you can incorporate the names of Allāh into your life, is by realizing the lessons that you gained from your hardships.

I personally went through hardships that have put me to the test many times, and midway I would realize that Allāh ﷻ is

certainly watching how I would handle this particular situation. I remember feeling the weight of my worries, and anxiety taking its toll on my consciousness. It was so heavy, that I began to slowly give up on the task that I wanted to pursue. I felt that if it was taking this long to get to where I needed to be, why should I even try. Perhaps, you can also relate to moments like this in your own life.

I found that I was sleeping more (so that I can sleep the pain away), I was also procrastinating my tasks in fear of failure, and I was also not taking care of my own self thinking that there is no way I can overcome and receive what I truly seek from Allāh ﷻ. These moments lasted a period of three days. I remember

thinking to myself on the fourth day, maybe this is all a test and I am failing miserably. Instead of allowing my soul to push through this heat, and come out the other side shining, I am keeping my soul in this dark place and forsaking it because of my own fears, impatience, and anxiety.

As humans we enjoy instant gratification, especially the youth in our generation. We want to be able to experience the finer things in life at a quick pace, and without any form of waiting or time. When time is involved we become hasty, and over think about the future instead of living in the moment.

So, in that moment, I thought to myself 'patience truly is a virtue'. For the past three days, I was so impatient with my circumstance, that it has sent me in downward spiral with my own mental and physical well-being. The virtue of patience is that it safeguards you from mentally falling into an endless spiral of despair. You train your heart and mind to see the beauty in the struggle and remain patience, with hope and aspiration that it will get better.

Patience is a virtue, it is hard, but truly it is a virtue. I thought to myself in that moment, of how Allāh ﷻ is *Al-Sabuur* (The most Patient). Many disregard Allāh ﷻ, many disbelieve in Allāh ﷻ, many forget to thank Allāh ﷻ, and many go as far as lying about our Creator.

Even so, He is the one who holds together the very particles that make up this universe – down to the simplest atom. He holds each atom, element, cell in your body, ordains every beat of your heart, and guides the steps you take over the earth. When you forget to pray, He doesn't forget to send rain from the heavens. When you forget to thank Him, He doesn't forget to bend light over your eyes so you could see.

So, who am I to be impatient about the things that happen to me in life? If anything, only Allāh ﷻ has the right to be impatient with us. But yet He remains gentle, composed, calm, and calculates His every move. You should teach your soul to be the same way. Allāh ﷻ could react instantly to the wrong we do and wipe us all out. Why do you have to react to every wrong done towards you? – Remain calm and envelope your soul with patience. Just like Allāh ﷻ, He is *Al-Sabuur* (the Patient);

surely you can be calculating and learn to take on the same gentleness in your own life, and watch as you grow in light and brilliance.

Learn to be calculating in the situations that life presents you, teach your mind to think twice about the opportunities you take on, the people you choose to be around, and the very interactions that you choose to have. Because this is your time, and you will never get it back. Spend it doing the things that will enrich you in the both worlds, and make sure that you treat your time like you do money. Money can be earned, but time cannot be earned once it is gone, it is gone. The most important winners in life are those who develop the art of time management from the very beginning.

They take on the trade by using their time on things and people that will benefit them, and not allowing people to waste it. The scene of the Day of Judgement will be one in which people will look back on their lives and wish that they lived it according to Gods plans. If only they did, then they would have made the correct life choices that would have made them find and befriend Him (Allāh ﷻ) before their final meeting with Him.

These people are the ones that will stand on the Day of Judgement hoping to go back.

They will see that the believers will have a light that is

surrounding them from their fronts, backs, and their sides. And they will ask, where did you get this light so that I can attain some of it. The believers will tell them, this light cannot be found right now and right here. This is a light that we accumulated on earth. Allāh ﷻ explains this scene in Surah Tahrim (The Prohibition) which is a chapter in the Quran. In these verses God says:

"O you who have believed, repent to Allah with sincere repentance. Perhaps your Lord will remove from you your misdeeds and admit you into gardens beneath which rivers flow [on] the Day when Allah will not disgrace the Prophet and those who believed with him. Their light will proceed before them and on their right; they will say,

"Our Lord, perfect for us our light and forgive us. Indeed, you are over all things competent." Quran 66:8

In another verse Allāh ﷻ says:

(On) the Day when the male hypocrites and the female hypocrites will say to the ones who have believed, "Look on us that we may adapt from your light!" It will be said to them, "Return (back) beyond you, so grope for a light!" Then a fence will be struck up between them, having a gate, in the inward whereof is mercy, and facing the outward thereof is the torment. The hypocrites will call to the believers, "Were we not with you?" They will say, "Yes, but you afflicted yourselves and awaited [misfortune for us] and doubted, and wishful thinking deluded you until there came the command of Allah. And the Deceiver deceived you concerning Allah." Quran 57:13-14

(By the way, the deceiver here means the shaytan (Satan), who was inviting them towards evil and keeping them away from good, thus causing them to waste their time on earth)

This light that the hypocrites and those who chose to disbelieve will beg for, will be one that the believers have. This light perhaps will be the very light that will allow believers to see through the darkness of the Sirat, and be able to pass through towards the passage to Paradise.

Since this light is something that you cannot get on the Day of Judgement, what is this light, and how can we attain it? We attain this light by the good that we do on this earth, it is the light that evelopes us and our souls. The light that we attain in this world can be seen by the angels of Allāh ﷻ. We cannot

physically see this light right now, but it will be seen on the day of Judgement. Many scholars say that this light is one that believers receive through making wudu (the ablution) for prayers. This light could also be the commitment you make towards the recitation of the Quran, it can accumulate through the charity work that you do, it is a light you receive based on the good that you do in this world.

Once your book of deeds close, and you head to the next world you can no longer do the deeds that will increase this light for you. So, do them now. Accumulate your light by the good work that you do, so that you can shine on the Day od Judgement when you stand before Allāh ﷻ.

If I can advise you anything in this world, it is to stick to the Quran and the Sunnah. To hold on as much as you can to the rope of Allāh ﷻ. If you have Him, you have everything that you need.

This world will push all of your energy towards it, but it is your responsibility to balance that energy and make time for your Creator. The true winners in life are those who make time for

Allāh ﷻ.

I want to emphasize some things that you can do to get closer to Allāh ﷻ. You can do this first by perfecting your prayers. When you do this, you will naturally see that disobeying Allāh ﷻ will slowly start to become distasteful to you. Obeying him will also become something that you look forward to. Try your best to make time for the Quran, remember, when you do this you are reading a message from the Creator of this entire universe. Each time you recite, and take the time to memorize the Quran you are elevated in status. The angels surround you as you recite the book of Allāh ﷻ, if you recite it fluently and without mistake. If you recite the book, but with difficulty, you will have double the reward.

The Prophet Muhammad (s.a.w) said, "Whoever recites the Qur'an secures knowledge of prophethood within his ribs [bosom], though Divine Revelation is not sent upon him. It does not befit one endowed with the Qur'an that he should be indignant with those in anger, nor should he indulge in any act of ignorance with those who are ignorant, while the Speech of Allah is there in his chest."

Source: Hakim, Targhib wa Tarhib no. 2/301 – [Sahih]

القرآنَ يعني منه خرج ممّا أفضلَ بشيءٍ اللهِ إلى ترجعون لا إنّكم

The Prophet Muhammad (s.a.w) said, "You will not come

back to Allah with anything better than that which came from Him, i.e. the Qur'an."

Source: Mastadrik al-Hakim no. 2077 - [Sahih]

<u>Let us look at some of the virtues of the Quran:</u>

Chapter: The Magnificence, Grandeur and Superiority of the Qur'an

1. The Prophet Muhammad (s.a.w) said, "The superiority of the speech of Allah compared to all other speech is like the superiority of Allah over His creation." Source: Tirmidhee no. 2926 - [Hasan]

2. The Prophet Muhammad (s.a.w) said, "Every Prophet was given miracles because of which people believed, but what I have been given is Divine Inspiration which Allah has revealed to me. So I hope that my followers will outnumber the followers of the other Prophets on the Day of Resurrection."
Source: Bukhari no. 4981, Muslim no. 152 - [Sahih]

The Prophet Muhammad (s.a.w) said, "Indeed Allah, through this Book, raises some peoples and lowers others." Source: Muslim no. 996 – [Sahih]

Chapter: The Level of Prophethood

3. The Prophet Muhammad (s.a.w) said, "Whoever recites the Qur'an secures knowledge of prophethood within his ribs [bosom], though Divine Revelation is not sent upon him. It does not befit one endowed with the Qur'an that he should be indignant with those in anger, nor should he indulge in any act of ignorance with those who are ignorant, while the Speech of Allah is there in his chest."

Source: Hakim, Targhib wa Tarhib no. 2/301 - [Sahih]

The Prophet Muhammad (s.a.w) said, "You will not come back to Allah with anything better than that which came from Him, i.e. the Qur'an."

Source: Mastadrik al-Hakim no. 2077 - [Sahih]

Chapter: Most Precise and Accurate

4. The Prophet Muhammad (s.a.w) said, "The most accurate and truthful speech is the Book of Allah [swt]" Source: Nisa'i no. 1578 - [Sahih]

The Prophet Muhammad (s.a.w) said, Allah [swt] said, "I have sent you [O Prophet] in order to put you to test and put those to test through you. And I sent the Book to you which cannot be washed away by water, so that you may recite it while in the state of wakefulness and sleep. Source: Hadith Qudsi, Muslim no. 2865a - [Sahih]

Chapter: The Qur'an is Pure and Undistorted

Ibn Abbas said, "How can you ask the people of the Scriptures about their Books while you have Allah's Book [the Qur'an] which is the most recent of the Books revealed by Allah, and you read it in its pure undistorted form?" Source: Bukhari no. 7522 - [Sahih]

Chapter: Reciting the Qur'an is a Light for You

The Prophet Muhammad (s.a.w) said, "It is imperative for you to have Taqwa [fear/consciousness of Allah] for this is the accumulation of all good. And upon you is Jihad in the path of Allah for it is the monasticism of the Muslims. [Finally]...upon you is the Remembrance of Allah and the recitation of His Book, for it is light for you on earth and [a means by which] you will be mentioned in the Heavens." Source: Targhib wa-Tarhib no. 4/24, Jami as-Sagheer no. 5495 - [Sahih]

Chapter: The Qur'an - an Intercessor

The Prophet Muhammad (s.a.w) said, "Fasting and the Qur'an will intercede for the slave on the Day of Judgement. Fasting will say, 'O My Lord! I prevented him from food and desires, so accept my intercession for him.' And the Qur'an will say, 'I prevented him from sleep during the night, so accept my intercession for him.' ....thus they will intercede."Source: Musnad Ahmad no. 6337 - [Sahih]

Chapter: The Qur'an as your Leader – guides you to Paradise. Placing behind your back leads to Hell

6. The Prophet Muhammad (s.a.w) said, "The Qur'an is an intercessor and it's intercession is accepted and its plea is believed. Whoever makes it lead him – it leads him to Paradise and whomsoever places it behind him [the result will be] he is

dragged to the Fire."Source: Ibn Hibban no. 124, - [Sahih]

Chapter: The Qur'an is a Proof/Evidence in your Favour or against You

The Prophet Muhammad (s.a.w) said, "Cleanliness is half of faith and Alhamdulillah [Praise be to Allah] fills the scale, and Subhan Allah [Glory be to Allah] and Alhamdulillah [Praise be to Allah] fill up what is be-tween the heavens and the earth, and prayer is a light, and charity is proof [of one's faith] and patience is a brightness and the Qur'an is a proof on your behalf or against you."

Source: Muslim no. 223 - [Sahih]

Often times we belittle ourselves so much, because we feel as if we are not good enough or perhaps compare our deeds to those of the prophets and the companions. The prophet Muhammad once mentioned the group of people whose faith is most astounding.

The Messenger of Allah ﷺ said, "Whose Faith [Iman] amongst the various creations astounds you?" They [the Companions] said, "The Angels" He said, "The Angels - Why would they not Faith [when they are with their Lord]" They [then] said, "The Prophets" He said, "The Prophets receive revelation so how would they not believe?" They [then] said, "[Us] the Companions" He said, "The Companions whom are with the Prophets - so how would they not believe? - However the Faith of people which is amazing and astounding is those who come after you who find Books which has written in them revelation [the Qur'an] - and hence they believe in it and obey and follow it - they are the ones whose Faith is [truly] astounding."

Source: Bazzar no. 3/318, Silsilah Ahadeeth as-Saheehah no. 3215 - [Sahih]

Let us understand Allah ﷻ in more depth by discussing the beginning of this universe:

The genesis of the universe is the sole beginning of all that there is now, and all that there was before. It was when God Almighty initiated the beginning of creation. What exactly was there before the creation of this great universe? Only God knows the detailed analysis to that question, this will be thoroughly investigated through evidence from the Quranic texts and Hadith (the Hadith are a collection of sayings from the Prophet Muhammad, which have been collected by his most trusted companions and passed down orally from generation to generation.). For those of you who do not believe in God, the answer to this will also forever remain a mystery. However, an abundant amount of scenes detailing this occasion is depicted to mankind in the Qur'an -- the last revelation to mankind. Before taking a look into these descriptions we must understand that Allah is independent of time. Therefore, concerning His Divine reality there is no before or after. According to the Quran Allah ﷻ reveals that He is the only Creator. Allah ﷻ, many times reiterates that He is the only Sustainer over the entire universe. His existence is not shaped by time or space, for that matter. Therefore, the Most High has no beginning nor an end. Out of the number of names that Allah exalts Himself with in the Quran, three of them are Al-Awal, Al-Akhir and Al-Samad; which mean -- the first, the last, and the eternal.

In terms of mans conscious intellect, time only exists when something exists. So as long as we exist, we will be completely wrapped within in the phenomenon of time. Thus, since time is the essence of our original nature it is much more easy for us to try to comprehend and relate the existence of Allah ﷻ with this limited measurement. We must know, the existence of the

Creator of this universe can not be measured. What Allah ﷻ

explains to us in His final revelation, is that time has a beginning

and an end. However, He who is the Creator of time does not

have a beginning or an end. He tells us that man who was

created along with time has a beginning and an end, but He

Exalted above man is Ever Existent and Ever Lasting.

For example ,mankind in our limited sense of the Divine Reality

might say, "there was a time when the universe didn't exist." In

reality what we should say is, "the universe didn't exist."

because the creation of time and the universe both come in the

same package; they are both the artistic forms of Allahs ﷻ

magnificent creativity that we will never be able to fully

understand. Thus, we know that if the universe does not exist

then time does not exist and vice versa. So the question is what was there before the subjectively perplexing aspect of time came into being? What we don't know for sure is if there was another universe like this one or perhaps a different realm. What we do know is that there was God. He was the first. So what exactly does Allah ﷻ say about Himself?

In the following verses Allah ﷻ reveals to all of mankind, the reality of His existence before He initiated the creation of time and the creation of this great universe. The most Merciful explains this relative to the realm of time -- in order that mankind might understand. The usage of His exalted names, "The First" and "The Last" are repeated to explain to us that; compared to His Creation He is "The First" but in general we must know that He is Ever-Existent, compared to His creation He is "The Last" but in general we must know that He is Ever-

Lasting. Thus the concept of time is only intertwined with the concept of Allahs ﷻ reality just for us to grasp and understand His nature relative to ours. That He is indeed Exalted above His creation.

"Say, "He is Allah , [who is] One, Allah the Eternal refuge." 112:1-2

"He is the First and the Last, the Outermost and the Innermost and He has full knowledge of all things," - The Qur'an, 57:3

"Allah - (there is) no God except Him, the Ever-Living the Sustainer of all that exists." The Quran 3:2 and 2:255

"And ever lasting will be the Face of your Lord, Owner of Majesty and Honor.(Surat Ar-Rahman 55:27)

When a man wants to send a letter to another individual. They must start with introducing themselves in a way that the one receiving his message can grasp who he is as a person. Therefore, the one revealing aspects about himself in the letter will explain accordingly, so that the receiver can understand. Otherwise the letter will be of no use and its message will not be able to properly get across. The same way in the Quran Allah ﷻ

Almighty, explains His characteristics in detail. This is so that we may understand, and get to know who our Creator is on a deeper level. So that we may know and understand what is it that Allah ﷻ the most High is pleased with, and is it that causes

His Divine anger.

"and We have revealed the Book to you explaining clearly everything" (16:89)

"And We sent down the book to you for the express purpose that you should make clear to them those things in which they differ, and so that it should be a guide and mercy to those who believe". (16:64).

So what does this tell us? Allah ﷻ explaining to us that He is the First and the Last, is relative to our existence. He is First compared to us. He is the last compared to us. However, He is also "Al-Samad" the ever-lasting. It gives a brief explanation of what we need to know about Allahs Divine Reality. By 'need', I mean what applies to us as human beings and what knowledge from the Almighty will benefit us for our temporary stay in this world. For example, asking questions such as "What was there before Allah?" we will never know, and it was never described to us in the Quran. What was explained to us in the Quran was the initiation of Creation; which is in fact knowledge pertaining to our origins and where we come from. This knowledge of our origin and the origin of the universe is of benefit to us. It is because upon knowing this reality we will be able to witness the Power of Allah ﷻ and appreciate His Might and Wisdom. All

aspects regarding our Creator and His reality beyond the creation of time and man is not necessary for us to know because that is pertaining to His Divine Being only. Anything pertaining to the realm of time and the creation of this universe has been explained in the Quran in detail (which will be covered later on). Of course what God explained to us in the Quran is only a fraction of His infinite knowledge. It is because of this that what we know is very little, and more importantly what we don't know is even greater.

Before understanding the Creation of the universe we must first familiarize ourself with its Creator. He has explained a numerous amount of his Exalted attributes in many parts of the Quran. One may ask, "so what is the wisdom behind these attributes of God?" Each and every one of these attributes are a sole part in Allah ﷻ being the Only True Creator and the only Deserving Creator of the worlds. As explained earlier, in order for a recipient of the letter to understand who its deliverer is; it must be explained within the letter. The message of the Quran is authored by the One and Only Creator. A significant feature of the Quran is that its verses often end with a pair of Allahs ﷻ attributes, names that describe His ultimate Sovereignty and Glory. Thus, the entire Quran is scattered with references of Allahs ﷻ personality. There will not be a page that one comes across without being overcome with a Divine characteristic of God. This is so that the reader of the Quran knows who their Creator, Sustainer and Fashioner is. So that, through our own limited characteristics we are able to grasp the Greatness of our Lord. The genesis of the universe begins with Allah ﷻ, so we must ask ourselves first; who is Allah?

Allah

"He is Allah, the One besides whom there is no other

deity, Knower of the unseen and the Witnessed. He is the most Merciful, the Compassionate. He is Allah, the One besides whom there is no other deity, the Sovereign, the Holy One, the Source of Peace, the Bestower of Safety, the Guardian, the Exalted, the Irresistible, the Supreme. Glory be to Allah above whatever they associate with Him! He is Allah, the Creator, the Maker, the Fashioner. To Him belong the beautiful Names. Whatever is in the heavens and whatever is on the earth glorifies Him, and He is the exalted, the Wise."

Qur'an [59:22-24]

The above verses stated by God Himself, is an explanation of the Divine nature of Allah the most High. These verses are in

Surah Al-Hashr; a chapter in the book of Allah called *The Gathering*.

Who is Allah (swt)? Allah ﷻ is the name of God. This name does not belong to any group, and it is not specified into any category. The name of Allah ﷻ is simply universal. It is the name that God has chosen for Himself. This is the name that has been uttered by the first man to walk this earth, the angels, prophets, messengers, and those who believed in the message and followed them. Each nation expressed the name of God according to the language God sent His revelation in. For example; in Armaic (the language of Jesus of Nazareth) the name for God was *Alaha*, in Hebrew (the language of David and Moses) the name for God was *Elohim*, and in Arabic (the language of Muhammad) the name for God was revealed as *Allah*. The similarity of Alaha, Allah, and Elohim lies in the fact that Hebrew, Arabic, and Armaic are closely related languages.

Until today people of many backgrounds, and languages who have accepted Gods way all across the world and developed this beautiful name into their language when speaking about God Almighty. Indeed, it is important to note that both Arab speaking Christians, Jews and Arab speaking Muslims refer to God as 'Allah' also. Allah ﷻ is the most Powerful, and he is infinitely most exalted than his creation.

The most-High is nothing like what He created, and remains unique to all that surrounds Him. The nature of the Almighty is so great and vast that it does not compare to any. The attributes of the Almighty is entirely ever existent, while the attributes of mankind are finite and are influenced by emotions, intellectual limitations, characteristic deviancy, and the social environment. Mankind is selfish, while Allah the most-High is Selfless. The Exalted Creator of this universe is not in need of His creation, rather the creation are in need of Him. God Almighty is dis-attached from emotions and is above all its influence. It must be understood that just because Allah (the most-High) is the most Merciful, it does not mean He will have Mercy on those who transgress against His commands. The most-High is a morally upright God, who is Just and Fair when given the circumstances and Loving and Merciful when given the circumstances.

Allah ﷻ is the Creator of heaven and its bliss, and He is also the Creator of Hell and its punishment. Since both of these realities were created by Allah the most-High, it will serve as the abode of whom it has been prescribed. Heaven is beyond our imagination and is beautiful in every way, therefore those who are deserving of its bliss will enter. Hell is the place in which the soul will be farthest from the grace of his Lord, condemned, and punished; therefore, those who are deserving of its punishment will enter. Although Allah ﷻ is eternally Merciful and Loving, His eternal Mercy will be enveloped around those who deserve the eternal Mercy and Love of their Creator. Consequently, since Allah ﷻ is Fair and Just, His Judgment will be either a swift brief punishment or a graceful eternity to those who will be deserving of either. In the final revelation to mankind the Highest describes Himself with many characteristics or attributes. These attributes are eternal, and often simultaneous through his ultimate Power and Will.

The attributes of Allah ﷻ (the Highest) are his characteristics

and the very nature of His being. Every single creation in this

universe exhibit their own way of personality and characteristic

traits that are unique from one another. Some people are more

patient than others in extreme circumstances, while others break

down in the face of adversity the moment it touches them. There

are people are very enduring and forbearing in the most

burdensome of situations, while others give up mentally and

spiritually the moment a dreadful situation arises in their lives.

Each and every creation of God are similar yet different in so

many ways. And so, these very characteristic traits that man was

created with is to show that a limited human can exhibit all of

these qualities, therefore the Creator of all that exists must be

One who has the ability to personify His own Divine attributes in any way He (the most High) wishes. These attributes were expressed in the Quran (the final message) in so many ways. This is in order that mankind understand their Originator and Maker, and have a firm idea of who their Creator is.

The way in which the Creator (most High Allah ﷻ) expresses His Divine attributes make sense. In order for a recipient of a message to understand where a letter came from they must be able to know who it is from. The Mercy of the Creator is such that, not only has He explained the final message is from Him but He also adds a detailed account of what we should know about His Divine Reality. And the Creator of the Children of Adam does this in a way where many verses end with two names that describe Him. Often verses in the Qur'an end with "...and He is the most compassionate, the most merciful", "...and

He is the most knowing, the most Wise", "...and He is the most High, the most Great", "...and He is the All-Hearing, the All-Seeing".

"Limitless is the Lord in His mercy..." Quran 6:147

The Power and Might of our Lord can be seen the moment a new born takes His first breath. It can be seen the moment the new born gains his first heartbeat in the womb of his mother. It is not the helpless newborn that has the power to form his heart or allow air to escape and return within the fold of his lungs; it is not the power of the newborn to choose its own mother, or be able to create his own mother, rather it is the Compassion of the most Merciful. The Almighty Lord is, the King of all Kings. All Governance, Power, Sovereignty and Might belongs to Him.

In the past text, we got to know who Allāh ﷻ is, His names

attributes, and how we can incorporate those names into our life.

Now we will learn about the nature of mankind and how the

story of the first man, Adam (peace be upon him) our father,

carries lessons that we can apply to our life today.

The Envy of Satan over Adam

When the story of Adam (peace be upon him) begins, Allāh ﷻ

starts by expressing the conversation that He (the most High)

had with the angels. Allāh ﷻ informs the angels about the

creation of Adam and that He will create a new entity that will

inhabit the earth and become the new leaders on earth. Notice, I said "new". Before this the first entities that inhabited the earth were the jinns and the demons, and the shaytan was the one who used to rule over them. This rulership of course, was one that Allāh ﷻ has given to Iblees (Satan) because of how good of a servant He was to our creator. Actually, Iblees (Satan) once had a high status with God (Allāh ﷻ) and because of this status He was entrusted to be among the angels in Paradise. Christians believe that He was a fallen angel (meaning he was once an angel and then transformed into a demon). Currently, many Muslims have confused the tale themselves, and started to believe that Iblees (Satan) was a fallen angel. That is not true. Iblees (Satan), was never an angel. He was a separate creation of Allāh ﷻ, that was created from fire. The angels on the other hand were created from light. It is important to know this difference because then people will believe that demons and angels have a relation to one another when they clearly do not.

That being said, Iblees (Satan) was given rulership of the lower earth and because of this rulership He was granted due to His proximity to Allāh some arrogance began to fester within him. The angels are a creation of Allāh ﷻ that do not have free will,

they follow the course of nature, and obey the commandments of Allāh because it is a part of their characteristic to do so. However, humans and jinns

(demons) have free will, and the choice to either commit to good deeds or bad deeds. Therefore, this is what separates angels from humans, and jinns.

Since the jinns were the first to inhabit the earth, the angels already had an idea of the pros and cons of the free will that was granted to them. They knew that when Allāh ﷻ would grant them free will, it entailed a form of power that they had, but they also had an idea that the power of free will had many disadvantages. The disadvantage being that they will one day be held accountable for the deeds that they committed amongst one another. That they will one day answer to these very deeds on the Day of Judgement.

When Iblees (Satan) found out that Adam and his children was the new inheritor of the earth, he began to grow in arrogance and deep jealousy. It is because of this that Iblees (Satan), promised to work hard to make all of mankind stray from the path of righteousness, and the one that will lead to paradise. We will touch more on this later but first I want you to understand the two things that happened before Allah ﷻ created Adam, our father (peace be upon him)

The First Testimony made by Humans:

When God first created the souls of every human, he held on to the souls that will one day inhabit the bodies we see on earth; and He said the following which is mentioned in the Quran:

When your Lord asked all the offspring of Adam (before their birth), "Am I not your Lord?" All of them testified and bore witness to their testimony that on the Day of Judgment they would not say, "We were not aware of this (fact)," Quran 7:172

This testimony is one that we made, and at that moment we had the awareness to be able to answer to this question. This of course cannot be remembered vividly, but Allāh ﷻ mentions that this testimony that we made when we were just our souls.

During the time of Prophet Muhammād ﷺ. The Jewish leaders would present to him certain questions that he must answer; in order to prove the legitimacy of his prophethood. .

There were many questions that they asked. Every time they asked him, Allāh ﷻ would instantly reveal to them the answer, in accurate detail. Each verse would begin, "…Tell them O Prophet…"

On many occasions, they accepted Islam due to how detailed

and historically correct the answers were. They thought, a man like Muhammād ﷺ , an Arab, could not be knowledgeable about our long lost history. .

Once they asked him about the Soul. This was the only question, they asked, that did not get a detailed response. Allāh ﷻ revealed, "…And they ask you about the soul, tell them, 'this is a matter only for Allāh." Qurān () This meant, no matter how detailed the answer, they can never imagine or understand the nature of the soul. Thus, they should leave this matter to Allāh ﷻ .

When Allāh ﷻ first created our souls, he gathered the soul of every human (during عالم الغيب – the world of the unseen). .

Our souls were presented with two promises. A Covenant and a Trust from Allāh ﷻ . We don't remember these occasions in our active conscious. But every human has something called the Fitrah, (like an a innate GPS) that allows us to remember.

Fitrah is the innate nature that drives human beings to worship. Once Allāh ﷻ presented the Covenant and the Trust to every soul, the Fitrah to worship Him and to Submit to His Will was activated in every human. This means even if you don't worship Allāh ﷻ , you are actively submitting to His will. How? By breathing. By your heartbeat. By the very blood that flows through your body. You have no choice but to follow the natural order, the natural laws of the universe. This *Fitra* (natural disposition), is a innate GPS-like system that every human has within their hearts, that drives them to worship. It causes every human to want to look for their purpose in life, find the reason for their existence, and search for their Creator. Although we do not vividly remember this moment, and the interaction that we once had with our Creator before we were born, we have a *fitra,* or a innate guidance system to causes us to yearn for the spiritual, a divinity to worship, and turn to. Hence why every human on earth is a slave to something. Many misunderstand why Allāh calls us humans a "slave" in the Quran. Many people in this world are slaves to their jobs, they are slaves to the companies they work for, slaves to the music industry, slaves to Hollywood, slaves to celebrities or famous entities they obsess over, or even slaves to chasing money and material things. Islam teaches that when you are slave to your Creator – you are devoting valuable time and energy into worshipping Him, instead of worldly things. The term "slave" has a very negative connotation because of human exploitation. However, when God (Allāh) uses this term, it denotes doing good work on earth, until we finally meet Him. We are doing the work on earth, and He is rewarding us for it with Paradise, which naturally makes us servants to Him.

Now, going back to the word *fitra*, Allāh describes this to us in the Quran in which He (the most High) says:

"So direct your face toward the religion, inclining to truth. [Adhere to] the *fitrah* of Allah upon which He has created [all] people. No change should there be in the creation of Allah. That is the correct religion, but most of the people do not know." Quran 30:30

What is this fitra that Allāh has created in all people, it is one that is inclining towards the truth. It is the part of the persons being that lights up as they read this book. It is the part of their being that feels at home when they hear and listen to the Quran (the Word of Allāh), it is a part of their being that recognizes the truth, and realizes the concepts of the truth. It is when their hearts soften to the truth, at that point it is up to them to be real to themselves and follow that truth. Those who have the chance to activate their *fitra*, and still reject the truth will stand in front of their Lord feeling at total loss.

Jinns, humans, and angels are created with this *fitra* (an inner being that inclines towards the truth). Angels naturally adhere to this *fitra*, while jinns and humans have to look for this fitra, or spend their life holding on to this *fitra*, and securing it with faith (iman). This *fitra*, the natural intellect within everyone to understand the truth, is a mercy from God. It is what allows people who were steered in the wrong direction because of their parent's faith (beliefs) – to find the truth. It is also the reason why there will be a Day of Judgement. Allāh will hold every human on earth accountable because they all had this *fitra*, (natural instinct to worship God), within them. It is up to each person to use their *fitra* to find the truth; which is monotheism, worshipping One God.

That being said, Iblees (satan) knew that he enjoyed a great status in the sight of Allāh, due to this He began to feel more and more proud of his position. When Allāh decided to create the first human, he told the angels that they would be the new inheritors of the earth. This story is mentioned in surah Saad, and surah Al-Baqarah, and surah Al-Ara'aaf.

In Surah Al-Baqarah (a chapter of the Quran), Allah mentions the following:

And [mention, O Muhammad], when your Lord said to the angels, "Indeed, I will make upon the earth a successive authority." They said, "Will You place upon it one who causes corruption therein and sheds blood, while we declare Your praise and sanctify You?" Allah said, "Indeed, I know that which you do not know." And He taught Adam the names - all of them. Then He showed them to the angels and said, "Inform Me of the names of these, if you are truthful." They said, "Exalted are You; we have no knowledge except what You have taught us. Indeed, it is You who is the Knowing, the Wise." He said, "O Adam, inform them of their names." And when he had informed them of their names, He said, "Did I not tell you that I know the unseen [aspects] of the heavens and the earth? And I know what you reveal and what you have concealed."

In Surah Saad (a chapter of the Quran), Allah mentions the following interaction between Him and the angels:

[So mention] when your Lord said to the angels, "Indeed, I am going to create a human being from clay. So the angels prostrated - all of them entirely. Except

Iblees; he was arrogant and became among the disbelievers. [Allah] said, "O Iblees, what prevented you from prostrating to that which I created with My hands? Were you arrogant [then], or were you [already] among the haughty?" He said, "I am better than him. You created me from fire and created him from clay." [Allah] said, "Then get out of Paradise, for indeed, you are expelled. And indeed, upon you is My curse until the Day of Recompense." He said, "My Lord, then reprieve me until the Day they are resurrected." [Allah] said, "So indeed, you are of those reprieved. Until the Day of the time well-known." Quran 38:71-81

The reality of a new creation being created angered Iblees (Satan), furthermore being told to bow down to this new creation, after his status was already elevated, was something that angered him. Out of arrogance, he said I am better than Adam, he is created from clay and I am created from fire. This was the first form of racism, or hatred ever expressed against a creation of Allah. This happens when one thinks that they are superior to another simply because of the way they were created. It is an act that also led to Iblees (Satan) being banned from

Paradise, and this is one of the many lessons we can take from this tale.

What we know for sure is the agenda that Iblees (Satan) has, is one that has been in the works for hundreds of thousands of years. It is one that he has worked hard to achieve, and that is to make sure that we never make it back to Jannah (paradise). Our purpose is to head back to our first origins, and that is in Jannah (paradise). The purpose of this first book, is to cover the importance that faith had in my life. All of this information that I shared in this book is the pre-requisite to the beautiful story you will read about in the next series. In life, there are many ups and downs, hurdles, and hardships that we come across and I have dealt with life changing moments in my own life that I will share in the next upcoming book. I will simultaneously weave in the tales of the ancient, lessons that I learned the hard way from spiritual insight, and how you can do the same. Until then, stay prayed up, and lock your hearts with the key of faith. May Allah always bless you, and may He give you everything you love if it is good for you and if it is not, I ask that He gives you what's best. Ameen. Asalamu' Alaikum Warahmatullah.

Printed in Poland
by Amazon Fulfillment
Poland Sp. z o.o., Wrocław

60532353R00085